Thriving

STEPPING INTO THE
LIFE YOU WANT

Thriving

STEPPING INTO THE
LIFE YOU WANT

...

Rebecca J. Morley

This book is my recycled pain and is for those like-minded souls who have even the smallest desire to be free.

I lovingly dedicate this book to the authors and healers who, over my many years of soul-searching and personal growth, offered me hope, perspective and a path to follow. My life is joyfully lived because of you and I am eternally grateful.

Thriving, like my life, is made possible because of good friends. To Chrissy, whose images give my words heart and to Gloria Eggert, whose editing give my words life, my gratitude is beyond words.

■ ■ ■

The best years of your life are the ones in which you decide your problems are your own. You do not blame them on your mother, the ecology, or the president. You realize that you control your own destiny.

Albert Ellis

contents

PART ONE Victim Mentality

PART TWO Taking Steps to a Thriving Life

PART THREE Encouragement for the Road Ahead

Preface

Dear Reader,

Writing this book has been a journey for me, and it is my delight to share it with you. It expresses what I've been through in my life and, often with the help of some wonderful authors, healers and mentors, explains how I've navigated my way to the life I truly want. The voices of those healers helped me until I could hear my own voice and start to help myself.

Though faith plays an important role in my life, you will not find religion here. To me faith unites us all. Please accept my words in the spirit in which they're offered, making good use of those concepts that resonate with you and simply leaving the rest.

I cannot begin to thank all the people who have supported me in this endeavor. It is honest to say that my life is truly a reflection of those who have sown so much love into me. I am honored to be a part of your journey!

With kindness and love,
Rebecca

Introduction

Similar to the labels we have on our clothing, we each wear internal labels. Your internal labels influence what you think and believe, how you act, and with whom you associate. Your internal labels ultimately determine your destiny. Two of the multitudes of internal labels we can wear are that of victim or thriver. This little book is about **thriving**.

I spent many years steeped in negative self-talk, procrastination, and constant disappointment. I was unable to find happiness or joy from within. I very much felt like a victim of my own circumstances. Maybe if I could make the world around me perfect, all the negativity and chaos in my head would disappear. But trying to create that perfect external world left me exhausted and further from my goal of a happy life. It felt like I was expending great effort to tidy up a sinking ship.

I found myself seeking pleasure, distracting myself from my real mission by pursuing any activity or behavior that gave me a quick lift. It worked for a while, but the results were empty and temporary, leaving me more disappointed and despondent. I felt frustrated, angry, and powerless to create the life I envisioned both internally and externally. I had lost hope that I could ever have the simple joy and happiness I so wanted.

I began exploring my internal labels, both personally and professionally, and I came to the conclusion that thriving is our most natural state. Thriving can be defined as the unlimited capacity for emotional and spiritual growth. It is living the best version of ourselves.

As a counselor, I feel great joy when I have the privilege of helping someone out of victimhood and into a thriving life. Each individual defines thriving differently, but nearly everyone would agree that a thriving life includes happiness and contentment. Many people find their happiness through authentic relationships, successful careers, or practices of inner peace. The difference between victimhood and thriving is simple. It is claiming your power to achieve the life you want. Moving from powerless to powerful is what this book is about.

No matter what you have been through or how long you've been stuck, this power for living and creating is found within you. This book will help you learn how to find and use that power. Through these exercises, you will be able to identify your internal labels, claim your power, change your thinking, and move into the life you want.

PART ONE
Victim Mentality

...

Revictimization and Self-victimization

■ ■ ■

We are all victims of something. Some of us have been sexually abused or raped, while others have experienced domestic violence, divorce, natural disasters, or racial prejudice. Victimization is also prevalent in our schools, where bullying throughout elementary school, middle school, and high school has, unfortunately, become more commonplace.

The initial act of sexual abuse, bullying, or any type of victimization is traumatic and, if identified, is generally addressed through counseling. In many situations, legal intervention may be necessary. Treated or not, hopelessness, helplessness, and shame (see appendix) can blossom from the seeds that were planted during the initial trauma, paving the way for chronic revictimization and self-victimization.

You might be asking, "Why would someone allow victimization to occur again, let alone self-victimize?" The answer is this: it is natural for human beings to seek comfort, and what is familiar brings comfort. For this reason, people tend to sit in the same seat on the bus or drive to work on the same roads. If you have been victimized, feeling bad is known territory. It is not that it is enjoyable; people who are stuck in patterns of victimhood instinctively sense that revictimization and self-victimization are not working to produce the life they want.

Change requires new behaviors. These new ways of being are unfamiliar and will feel uncomfortable. In seeking comfort, they unknowingly revert to recreating what they know: being victims. This is the cycle that needs to be broken.

Revictimization occurs when a person is abused again and again. Those who are revictimized may leave one abusive situation only to enter another in which they

are treated poorly. Though the victims are unaware, they are triggered to respond to the current abusers as they did to the initial abusers. This brings another comfortable and familiar, yet negative, situation into the victims' lives.

Self-victimization is a bit more difficult to spot because the abuse is hidden from the victim, by the victim. Feeling bad is perceived as normal and therefore comfortable. Negative thoughts deliver the "comfortable" bad feelings that have become the victim's way of being.

The hallmark of self-victimization is when victims unconsciously allow negativity to dominate their thoughts. Devaluing thoughts and name-calling such as "stupid" or "failure" are further evidence of self-victimization. Predictions of a bleak future are common because, at some level, self-victimizers believe they don't deserve to feel good. In this situation, the victims have become their own abusers.

No one wants to be a victim; the word *victim* is often associated with weakness. But victims feel as if they have no control, that they cannot stop the pain, and that they are trapped in victimhood.

I have been blessed to travel this healing journey with many people through my work in community mental health, child welfare, juvenile justice, private practice and hospice. I am witness to the destruction that happens to those who are victims of abuse and their families. Some of the most significant work I do is to counsel those victims. It is common for the victims to assume the blame for the abuse. Because they are told it is their fault, they come to believe that this must be so. The unbelievable horror of the situation has the victims trying to make sense of what makes no sense at all. They have been hurt and abused and feel responsible at the same time. Long after the abuse has stopped, they are trapped in a life of pain that they neither want nor understand.

Victimization is not our natural state, and no one wants to feel used or trapped. While it is not possible to go back in time and change the initial victimization, it is possible to do something about the pain coming from revictimization and self-victimization.

People experiencing revictimization and self-victimization often report a wide range of symptoms and behaviors, including depression, anxiety, chronic illness, eating disorders, relationship issues, career challenges, exhaustion, and various addictions. These individuals identify so much with their pain that they begin to see themselves as merely a collection of their wounds. The world they see is distorted, resulting in a state of being that is referred to as *victim mentality*.

victim-mentality checklist

■ ■ ■

DO YOU...

- ☐ say "I can't"
- ☐ hate yourself
- ☐ blame others
- ☐ feel resentful
- ☐ expect to fail
- ☐ make excuses
- ☐ mistrust others
- ☐ lack confidence
- ☐ often feel angry
- ☐ want to be rescued
- ☐ have negative self-talk
- ☐ feel extreme negativity

- ☐ feel shameful
- ☐ try to be perfect
- ☐ expect the worst
- ☐ sabotage yourself
- ☐ apologize frequently
- ☐ feel guilty all the time
- ☐ have constant self-doubt
- ☐ frequently ask "Why me?"
- ☐ take too little responsibility
- ☐ have extreme expectations
- ☐ feel chronic disappointment
- ☐ take too much responsibility

Do you see yourself in the above list? Individuals with victim mentality often describe feeling trapped or stuck, as if they have no power to change.

But there is hope. This book is here to offer that hope—hope for change and hope for a better life. Change is possible when you understand the process and become willing to take action. Reading this book is that first step into action!

The Two parts of victim mentality

. . .

Victim mentality has two parts. The first part is the lie that is believed, and the second part is the excuse that supports the lie. These two parts keep us stuck in a life we no longer want. A person with victim mentality has self-talk that may sound like this:

> "I can't do (**the lie**) because (**the excuse**)."

Let's start by looking at some common excuses that keep us stuck in victimhood:

> "My mother was abusive to me."
> "I don't have enough money."
> "My spouse cheated on me."
> "I was sexually abused."

The excuse is who or what we blame, otherwise known as scapegoats. It is common to have a pen of scapegoats, but everyone has a favorite (your mother-in-law, your spouse, your abuser, or other persons or situations). While our scapegoats go on to live their lives, we torment ourselves by ruminating on what they did or did not do or say. We stop living our own lives, choosing instead to focus on our scapegoats. When we consistently choose to feed our scapegoats, we give up control of our lives. We lose our personal power, and positive change becomes impossible.

What are the names of your scapegoats? If you are unsure, take a moment and ask yourself a few questions. Is your life where you want it to be? If not, what person or situation do you believe is responsible for the state of your life? This little exercise may reveal that you have a scapegoat(s) that you believe is holding you back. You are basically saying, "I don't have the life I want because of them." When you release the scapegoat, you are actually setting yourself free—free to create the life you want.

Examples of Victim Mentality

■ ■ ■

"I can't stop drinking because it is the only way I can deal with the stress of my unhappy marriage." Using this excuse, the victim continues to drink and blames that action and its consequences on his or her spouse.

"I can't lose weight. I'm trapped in working long hours to compensate for my spouse's low-paying job and have no time to take care of myself." Using this excuse gives the victim license to continue behaving in ways that support being overweight by blaming that fact on his or her spouse.

"I can't go to work again today! I'm just too upset because of the fight I had with my child." This person is less likely to get a promotion or raise because of poor attendance but, instead of taking personal responsibility, assigns blame to his or her child.

Once you examine your life and understand how and where you are using scapegoats, you are ready to look at the first part of victim mentality, which is the lie. The lie is the "I can't" part of your life.

Some things truly cannot be changed, such as your past, your genetics, and the reactions of other people. These require you to lovingly accept those people or circumstances, a process that is often harder than working on the things that can be changed.

Take a moment to identify things in your life that need to be accepted. Specifically, what is beyond your control as it applies to your circumstances? What will you not be able to change no matter how hard you try? Whatever just popped into your mind, that thing, right there, is the very thing you must accept. Find peace in the acceptance of this reality.

Then you will be ready to focus on what you can change *in the present*, which will ultimately affect your *future*.

PART TWO
Taking Steps to a Thriving Life

■ ■ ■

Taking Steps to a Thriving Life

∎ ∎ ∎

The next question is obvious:
What can I change?

There was a time when the pain in my life indicated that something needed to change. I had no idea how to begin. I found myself in a challenging relationship with my aging mother. I was clinically obese and chronically disappointed, and I lived with a checkbook that hadn't been balanced in many years. There was no task in my world that I could complete. I was totally out of control, and I had no idea why. But all the while, I looked functional to the outside world. I successfully held a job, and I seemingly took decent care of myself—but I knew better inside.

My entire world shifted when I grasped the concept espoused by motivational pioneer Louise L. Hay in her book, *Meditations to Heal Your Life*, "...beliefs are only thoughts, and thoughts can be changed." The "I can't" thought was my default position. I really believed I didn't have the ability to take charge of my own life. I realized that "I can't" was masking what I really thought: "I don't want to," "I'm afraid," or "I don't know how."

I now know that it is rarely true that "I can't." It is an erroneous belief. In truth, the "I can't" thought is like any other thought—it can be changed. If I believe that something is impossible, I've made it impossible *for me*. But when I dared to believe that my life could be different, it truly transformed.

Some thoughts that lead to a thriving life might be the following: "I *can* lose weight."
"I *can* support myself."
"I *can* get my book published."
"I *can* better my education or job."
"I *can* be free of drugs and alcohol."

Just as there are two parts to the problem—the lie and the excuse—there are two parts to the solution. You must let go of the lie ("I can't") and let go of the excuse (blaming your scapegoat) that is keeping you engaged and holding you back. Accepting that your current life condition is not your scapegoat's fault frees you up to start saying, "*I can!*"

Every time you say "I can" you are making yourself stronger. Every time you release a scapegoat, you are lighter and freer. The two ideas work together because when you say "I can" you are choosing to disengage from your scapegoats, liberating yourself to step into your own life.

Your desire for positive change must be followed by action because desire without action is just wishful thinking. This

work can be challenging, but doing nothing absolutely assures that you will remain a victim.

Not everyone who reads this will be ready for change. Some individuals have been so beaten down that they have become addicted to the chaos and drama in their lives. I believe they want to change but are not yet ready. If you're ready, however, know that your life will change dramatically as you take steps away from victimhood toward thriving. Not everyone in your life will be ready to accompany you on your journey. It takes courage to move on, and equal courage to leave behind those whose journeys differ from yours.

Now that you have defined your problem with the help of the Victim-Mentality Checklist, let's get to the solution!

Below are some practical principles to get you started on your way to a thriving life. You don't need to tackle them all at once. Not everyone will begin at the same spot. So see what strikes you as true, and get going! Change may be slow at first, but be encouraged that any forward movement is progress toward your goal.

I want to encourage you to step away from your painful beliefs (your lies) and take personal responsibility by doing a few items from the list. I know this for certain: changing your thoughts leads to changing your behavior; changing your behavior leads to changing your thoughts. Each is supportive of the other, and either can begin the positive cycle of change. Remember: action is necessary for any change to take place. Here is where you can find your first steps toward your thriving life.

Thinking Differently

■ ■ ■

Realize that beliefs are just thoughts, and thoughts can be changed.
According to Louise Hay's influential teachings, you do not have to think, believe, or feel the way you currently do. You can change your thinking. There are always options. That thought you are thinking right now, no matter how negative, that thought can be changed—and you have the power within you to do it!

Practice forgiveness toward those who victimized you.
Harboring resentment toward those who hurt you is like drinking poison and expecting them to die. As the people you resent go on with their lives, your resentment will continue to harm you, keeping you weak and barring you from living your thriving life.

Forgiving your abusers lets you out of your self-imposed prison. When you forgive, the importance of the abusive situation is so diminished that it no longer fuels your life. Lack of resentment is your indicator that you've forgiven and are free. This doesn't have to be forced. Sometimes the first step is simply the willingness to forgive.

Practice self-forgiveness.
Some students asked their yogi master about the difference between him and them. His reply was simple: "I practice self-forgiveness all day long." Replacing patterns of blaming and general negativity with the kindness of self-forgiveness supports our souls and frees up time and energy for creating the positive lives we want.

Accept that no person, government, or job is responsible for your health, success, happiness, and well-being.
I am responsible for those things. I need to consciously make daily choices to produce the life that I want. I have stopped looking outside myself for my own happiness. This daily practice allowed me to become my own champion. You can do it too!

Give up the need to be right.
Being right can be a lonely place. Being right only feeds your ego and provides a temporary satisfaction. When you give up the need to be right because kindness has become more important, you will be on the path to real satisfaction. There is genuine joy in setting aside your needs to extend kindness to another. This is where your highest self resides.

Explore humility and equality.
Thinking that you are better than others creates division, leaving you feeling separated and isolated. Likewise, thinking that you are less than others also creates division, leaving you feeling separated and isolated.

True humility is feeling no better and no worse than your peers. You are equal. This is called being right-sized. Right-sized individuals live in community with others and share feelings of belonging and satisfaction.

Let go of black-and-white thinking.
Black-and-white thinking shrinks your world down to only two options: right or wrong, good or bad. Black-and-white thinking is a normal response to a limiting environment that was imposed upon us in childhood.

When brought into adulthood, black-and-white thinking judges that we are happy when people and situations are good/right and unhappy when people and situations are bad/wrong. The trap with this type of thinking is that nothing and no one is ever all good or all bad.

When we judge ourselves with a black-and-white perspective, we tend to judge others by that same measure. It's the rare relationship that can survive this sort of rigidity. When black-and-white thinking is surrendered, the world opens up to a variety of colors and options. Satisfaction and happiness are found in "good enough."

Stop labeling events as good or bad.
Events are neutral. How you choose to view them labels them as good or bad. If you label the event as good, it leads to happiness. If you label the event as bad, it leads to dissatisfaction and sadness. Many events in our lives are best framed as opportunities.

Let go of regret.
Regret is defined as chronic remorse. When you say, "I should have…" you're believing that a different decision would have resulted in a more favorable outcome. Give no energy to past decisions that cannot be changed. When the outcome is not what you want, it is important to know that you have the power to improve the situation by simply making another decision. Instead, choose to move forward with your new decision.

Believe in abundance in the universe.
Thoughts of lack and scarcity only attract more lack and scarcity. If you believe you will have less of anything, be assured you will have less. If you hold the belief that there is more than enough of everything to go around, you will relax and enjoy all you need or want. For instance, if you think there is not enough air for you to breathe, you will tense up and tighten your muscles against the lack of air. But if you relax, believing you can breathe easily because the air is all around you, you will. The same is true of love, money, time, talent, beauty, and good health. If you truly believe these things are yours, they are.

Explore the mind-body connection.
Your thoughts have the ability to make you physically sick or boost you to good health. View your physical challenges as reflections of your current level of thinking. Do you really want to hold those negative thoughts when you know they could contribute to ill health?

Turn things around.
All challenges are opportunities to practice a positive point of view. Is your negative mother bringing you down, or can you smile and choose to see her as giving you the opportunity to practice acceptance and grow stronger in your own positive outlook?

See truth as valuable.
When someone points out something painful, take a moment to look for the nugget of truth. When your coworker makes a comment about how much you gossip, it will sting. The sting, your pain, comes from knowing that there is an element of truth in the comment. It takes maturity to look past your pain and consider that truth. That truth is your stepping-stone to becoming the person you want to be.

Pain is not your enemy.
We do not like to be uncomfortable or have emotional pain. We all know what it feels like when the slightest comment triggers that pain.

Experiencing such pain is like your body contracting a virus and developing a fever as a way of combating it. Your body is letting you know it's sick and needs help.

Emotional pain is actually our internal feedback mechanism that lets us know that our healing is in progress. Grabbing a substance or hiding in an activity to remove or blunt the pain stops us from moving forward and invites the pain to show up again.

Be patient with your own growth.
We are innately designed to grow and improve throughout our lives. Often we are motivated to start our journeys because we are experiencing pain. I understand wanting to be out of pain *now*. We live in a society where instant gratification is almost an expectation.

Rarely do we change overnight. Being at peace with the daily process of growth requires patience. This is not a timed race. Be kind and supportive to yourself. Your goal is to simply acknowledge and celebrate each insight and victory as you move toward health. Those small victories really do add up.

Give up the idea that more is better.
More things (food, money, or clothing) will not give you the peace you are looking for. Studies show that people do not have joy because they have things. You can be joyful regardless of your possessions and perceived status. Peace and happiness come when you choose to actively practice gratitude for what you already have.

Get past your anger with God.
Deep, scarring wounds can leave us bitter or resentful that someone or something allowed this to happen to us. Wounds are made sacred when we transform them into a source of power and well-being, going from bitter to better. For instance, your career choice may be a direct reflection of the pain you've experienced. A battered child may choose to work in the criminal-justice system or find fulfillment as a therapist.

Today, I am clear that my sacred wounds put me in the counseling field where I can recycle my past experiences into positive help for others. As we let go of old hurts, we become the best version of who we were meant to be. Your adversity and pain are your biggest blessings, and you can actually grow to be thankful for those wounds.

Behaving Differently

. . .

Change your language.
Develop and use "I choose" and "I can" language rather than continuing to tell yourself, "I'm helpless," or "I can't." You *can* leave that terrible job or abusive spouse. You *can* stop drinking. You *can* change your life, so start talking like you *can*!

Write your unique mission statement.
Develop your life purpose by writing a mission statement that will guide and direct your choices, activities, and friendships. When you are lost, return to your personal mission. Sir Richard Branson, founder of the Virgin Group, has the unique mission statement that reads, "To have fun in my journey through life and learn from my mistakes."

My mission statement is "to be a healing force in the lives of others by seeing and revealing their greatness while being authentic to myself."

Be a fan club member.
Look inside, and unleash your natural capacity for understanding and kindness, which we all have. Being kind is clearly easier for some and can be considered their superpower. Other superpowers can include anything from being a quiet, focused listener to having persistent willingness to help others in their time of need. When you

acknowledge the superpower of others with kindness and respect, they can see their gifts through your eyes. The act of noticing and speaking the good you see in others also gives you the language to be a fan club member for yourself.

Live in the present.
As you come to understand that *now* is truly all you have, you have a daily opportunity to show up differently in every situation you encounter. This concept is known as *mindfulness*. Mindfulness draws your focus back from the past and away from the future into the now. Ask yourself the question: How is my now? When my daughter was four, she answered: "My now is great!" That's my focus every day.

Get physical.
Make exercise part of your life. Exercise elevates the mood, decreases anxiety, provides an outlet for stress, and improves overall health.
Whether you choose to participate in classes or games or to exercise on your own, whatever engages you is the activity you should do. Give yourself the gift of movement! You will find that exercise benefits every part of your life.

Set clear boundaries.
Give yourself permission to say no at times. There are so many opportunities and ways to spend your time. There are always good causes to support and various needs to be met. That doesn't mean these automatically become yours to do, even when you're invited. It's important to not set yourself up to do things you really don't want to do.

Doing what you don't want to do just to please others has you bringing an unhappy person to the party. If you have trouble saying no, then create space by saying, "I'll get back to you on that." Honor yourself, your time, and your energy. Once you know your truth, offer a happy yes or a polite "No, thank you."

Look for life teachers.
Find someone who has experience helping others with your particular issues. Be open to ideas you have never considered. There are various life teachers you can learn from. Take notice of those who espouse the life you seek. Asking their guidance will help you find healing practices that you can incorporate into your own life. That first teacher is your stepping-stone to others who will further enrich your journey.

Focus on doing the right thing.
This means letting go of what you think others will think of you and choosing instead to spend your time and energy doing the right thing. Stop trying to manage your reputation. When you do the right thing, your reputation will take care of itself.

Make Amends.
Making amends requires you to first increase your level of awareness of your impact on your world and the people in it. Once aware of the hurt you can cause, no matter your intention, you can take action to clean up the wreckage. Amends can include righting a misdeed, apologizing for your hurtful words, or paying back an old debt. When you've done the right thing, you'll be amazed at how quickly your spirit lightens, and you can let it go.

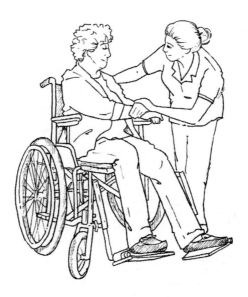

Make a living amends.
Living amends is the step beyond the apology. It is quite literally choosing to behave differently. We change what we do and how we do it. We choose to become the best versions of ourselves each day. As we seek a thriving life, we can choose to treat ourselves and others with more respect. Living amends restore our relationships. When we live in awareness and stop creating new wreckage, life is so much better.

Recycle your pain.
Recycle your pain by helping others. Dealing with your own pain puts you in a unique position to offer understanding and compassion to others. Become a safe place for others to rest their weary, hurt souls. Be a good friend, or volunteer at a domestic-violence shelter, at a hospice, or for some other cause that touches your heart.

Use positive affirmations.
The words we say to ourselves hold great power. You are not ugly or incapable, but you believe you are because that is what you were told. Positive affirmations declare what is true. You are worthy of love. You are a good person. You are a person of value. Make affirmations a big part of your daily self-talk.

Practice rest.
Build rest into your life. Taking responsibility takes energy, and rest will bring replenishment. You may rest by taking a short nap on your lunch hour or giving yourself permission to not attend that extra event.

Practice stillness with meditation.
Meditation slows us down and brings us into the present. Since many people with victim mentalities experience depression and anxiety, meditation is an especially beneficial tool. *Depression* is that helpless feeling of being stuck in the past, while *anxiety* is being stuck in

fretful anticipation of the future. The act of meditating brings you into the present by removing distractions and worries and focusing your mind in the present moment.

Dr. Joe Dispenza, international lecturer, researcher, corporate consultant, author and educator states, "The main purpose of meditation is to remove your attention from the environment, your body, and the passage of time so that what you intend, what you think, becomes your focus instead of these externals." He further clarifies that "meditation is a time in which you prune away old ineffective behaviors and envision new effective behaviors which allows you to step into your new personal reality."

There are many people teaching meditation today. I encourage you to find someone whose teaching resonates with you. The positive effects of meditation are virtually limitless, but the benefits are only available to those who put this discipline into practice.

Let go of asking why.
Stop looking for the reasons behind life events and other people's behavior. We often believe that understanding will lead to peace. When you ask why, you judge that things should be another way. Judging pulls you back into the victim mentality of good/bad, right/wrong. In reality, the peace you seek comes from taking action or finding acceptance.

Avoid emotional procrastination.
Putting off that difficult conversation with a loved one or coworker takes enormous energy as you continue to ruminate on the situation in your mind. The longer you procrastinate, the worse the situation becomes. Each time you review it in your head, you validate and strengthen your sense of victimhood. Learn to say what you need to say quickly and kindly so that you can get on with your life.

Ask for help.

Columnist Rona Barrett said, "The healthy and strong individual is the one who asks for help when he needs it. Whether he's got an abscess on his knee or in his soul." Many people find it difficult to ask for help because they have to admit that they can't do this on their own—and they feel weak or embarrassed. It takes humility to ask for and accept help. There is benefit in acknowledging your humanity, allowing yourself to be helped by another, and moving past that place of being stuck. Humble up, and ask for help.

Live by laws.

We all adhere to the physical law of gravity because it is imposed upon us. We choose to live by ethical laws to avoid harming ourselves or others, such as not drinking and driving. You can choose to live by spiritual laws like forgiveness, kindness, charity, and goodness. These and other such laws plant good seeds in the universe and bring flavorful fruit to all.

Use music.

Down in the dumps? Turn on some music. Along with exercise and meditation, music remains one of the most powerful tools for improving mood and shaping outlook. There are several songs and artists that have this impact on my soul, and it only takes choosing to hit the play button to turn things around. Find your song.

Aim your anger in the right direction.

We are often angry when we don't get our way or when we think we have been taken advantage of. We cannot resolve our anger until we clarify at what or with whom we are angry. If you are boiling hot because your friend made you late for the tenth time, I encourage you to look at yourself. Are you angry with your friend for being late or angry with yourself for allowing this situation to occur yet again? Accepting that your friend cannot be on time sets you free to make another plan that allows you to arrive peacefully and on time.

Create a support system.
Support comes in many different shapes and sizes. Attend a twelve-step support group or a community support group that offers help on a wide array of life-management topics. Get a sponsor, a mentor, or a friend on a similar path who will love you until you can love yourself. That person can share your journey, offering support and mutual accountability.

Pursue professional support.
Pursue healing with a professional counselor or coach when needed. Find someone you feel comfortable with, and get to work. Select someone who is forward thinking. I healed more quickly when I was engaged in the "what and how" than when I was looking back and asking why. "Why" kept me anchored in the victim role.

Be generous.
Generosity means extending yourself beyond your normal way of being and comes in many versions. There is financial generosity, emotional generosity, and generosity of spirit.

Generosity is that open-hearted attitude that says, "I'm not diminished by giving to you." In fact, the opposite is true. Your life is enlarged by giving to others. The act of giving is an expression of love. Giving love positively impacts the recipient, who is likely to reflect it back on you or pass it on to others, creating an ever-renewable supply.

Enjoy laughter.
When we are in emotional pain, we are often serious. There is great benefit in not taking ourselves so seriously. Seek out humor, and invite it into your life. Laughter, like meditation, is powerful. Forcing yourself to smile when your spirit says otherwise has been proven to create those feel-good brain chemicals, endorphins, and actually improves your mood. Take time to smile and laugh today!

Practice radical gratitude.
Regular garden-variety gratitude happens when we're thankful for something that we have been given. Radical gratitude, however, is out-of-the-box thinking.

There are two ways to practice radical gratitude. The first is to anticipate the future with a grateful heart. It is the assumption that all will be well. Decide to be thankful for whatever comes your way.

The second way to practice radical gratitude is by choosing to be thankful for a difficult situation or person in your life. I'm sure you've experienced something that seemed negative at first but ultimately turned out to be a really good thing. Though it might seem unreasonable to be grateful for something negative, new insights and opportunities are often the unexpected gifts of challenging situations.

I encourage you to be grateful for your difficult boss or other uncomfortable circumstance. Your difficult boss could be offering you a roadmap to who you might choose to be instead or might be teaching you diplomacy. Any uncomfortable situation can point you to what you might need to change in your own life. Gratitude allows you to see your situation differently. When something negative happens and you say thank you, change happens. Sometimes the change occurs in you. Sometimes the change occurs in the situation. Either way, cultivating gratitude works!

Every day, choose to be thankful for something or someone. Be radical and include all the negatives along with the positives. You'll soon notice your attitude changing, your spirits lifting, and the new benefits of radical gratitude appearing in your life.

Give up multitasking.
Enjoy the discipline of doing one thing at a time and doing it well instead of taking on multiple tasks and doing them poorly. Remember the old adage "the hurrier I go, the behinder I get!" Going faster and trying to do more kills the fun and creates emotional mayhem, weariness, and inefficiency. It's really worth finding the joy in single-tasking.

Don't take on extra weight.
People who are hurt often blame others. Are you being blamed? Are you guilty of some misbehavior or thoughtless word? If you are, be aware of how you contributed to the situation, and

set things right. If you aren't, assume no responsibility. Know that making others feel better is not your job. Be your best person, and acknowledge others' feelings by offering a kind word like, "I'm sorry you feel bad." It's important that you not take the extra weight of their unhappiness with you on your journey.

Declutter your environment.

The management of *stuff* can keep you so busy that there is no time for emotional change. Keep only those things that bring you joy and enhance the quality of your life. Decluttering will simplify your life, leaving you room to breathe and energy to work on those things that really matter. And there is joy in blessing another individual or organization with those items you no longer need. Check online for charitable organizations near you.

Label your journey.
It helps to give your journey a name. Making it a fun name is even better: *Mystic in Training, Practitioner of Radical Gratitude, Jedi Warrior Seeking Peace*—whatever silly or nonsensical phrase makes you smile and gives you focus will help you remember your mission.

Review your inner circle.
It is said that we become like the five people we spend the most time with. Take a look around. Is your inner circle filled with negativity, judgment, sarcasm, and scarcity? Seek out the happy people who have what you want, and spend more time with them. You will begin to look more like them as you emulate their behaviors.

Practice the acceptance of others.
Take the energy you were spending on trying to change others and use it to change yourself. Everyone is on a personal journey. If you stay on yours while honoring theirs, acceptance is easier. In difficult moments, you can summon that classic prayer: "Bless them; change me."

Learn what is toxic.
When you are exposed to a toxic substance, a negative reaction is normal. These responses can range from a simple upset stomach or rash to death. Just as reactions to physical toxins are normal, it is equally normal that situations and people can be toxic to us. Exposure to emotional toxicity also has a range of reactions. You may feel anger, confusion, or simply that sense of being unsafe. It is important to identify situations or individuals that we find toxic.

When I let go of a toxic relationship, I also had to give up the good things that person brought into my life. Today, I avoid even a little bit of toxicity.

Build routine into your life.
Structure and routine do not make your life boring. They provide a consistent, safe place in which you can pursue your growth. To begin, try going to bed and getting up at the same time each day. Make meditation a daily practice. Do things that build a reliable foundation upon which your spontaneous activities can rest.

Practice awe.
Being in a state of awe is the most magical of experiences. When we pause and absorb something of sheer beauty with any of our senses, we are gifted with moments of amazement that lift us above the mundane. We can view our lives from a higher perch and breathe in the invigorating newness that is offered. Now that I am fully open to the experience, I choose to see the moments of awe in the life I have.

Find the good.
Look hard, and find the good in every situation—including that flat tire or the death of a loved one. Sometimes the good is not easy to find. When that's the case, trust that it is present and has yet to be revealed to you. It may be easier for a friend to see and point out to you. Mizuta Masahid, seventeenth-century Japanese poet and samurai, said it best when he wrote, "Barn's burnt down—now I can see the moon."

Listen to yourself.
We all have an inner voice. This voice can be as simple as an internal inkling or an undeniable knowing. Victims often bury their voices and believe and act on the voices of others above their own.

Early in my healing, my internal voice gave questionable advice. That's why I have mentioned the healers who were so invaluable to me. Once my victim mentality began to subside, I started looking within for my answers. Today, I practice being quiet and seek that place of knowing for my answers. When I am challenged, I need friends who will walk me through my uncertainty until I find my truth.

Pursue the divine.
Above all, cultivate a relationship with the divine, your God, whatever you consider to be your life source. You can seek this relationship through reading, meditation, prayer, or organized religion. You will gain remarkable benefits from recognizing that you are not alone and that there is a power greater than you that is willing to carry your burden and illuminate your path.

Never, ever give up.
Children between the ages of six and twelve often tell me about fearful images that come into their minds at night while they're trying to fall asleep. I encourage them to change the images as if they were changing a TV channel.

They report that when they try the exercise, the fearful images return. I then explain that they need to flip the channel to the good place as many times as necessary.

This exercise works for adults too! Ruminating over your problems, indiscretions, angers, and resentments offers you the same opportunity to change the channel. First, making your thoughts go back to the positive again and again shows you that you can condition your mind to push back the negative and choose the positive. Second, if you don't give up, you will eventually see results. In the beginning, you may need to change the channel forty times. As you continue this practice, you'll find yourself more naturally opting for the positive channels and the good feelings they affirm. Motivational speaker Jim Rohn said it well: "Motivation gets you started; habit is what keeps you going."

PART THREE
Encouragement for the Road Ahead

■ ■ ■

Encouragement for the Road Ahead

. . .

The biggest lie that we tell ourselves at one time or another is the lie, "I can start tomorrow." Change requires work, and it can be uncomfortable or painful. A part of our being wants to avoid discomfort and will sabotage our efforts with that lie, "I can start tomorrow."

I believe we can do anything if we can overcome the fear of being uncomfortable. It helps to remember that there's a "woo-hoo!" on the other side of the discomfort. I encourage you to endure the momentary discomfort of change to get the life you want.

I understand that sometimes we want something or someone to blame (scapegoats). I recently had a particularly fearful task in front of me. My first reaction was to chase down an old scapegoat and haul him back to my pen to blame. That only tortured me, making me feel weak and miserable, creating a desire to indulge in old behaviors that are not good for me. Thankfully, I have a great support system and a mentor who always tells me the truth while offering love and support. I've also adopted the disciplines of meditation, prayer, and exercise that always return me to my center. I released the scapegoat and went on with my task. I was able to complete the task that frightened me, and my energy and serenity returned.

As you start to say, "I can," and release your scapegoats, your focus reorients, and you may notice subtle changes. You might start saying no when you don't want to do something. You might ask for a transfer to get away from a difficult work situation. You will find that you no longer refer to yourself in negative terms. You might catch yourself feeling lighthearted and even laughing more. The perfectionism you required of yourself and others has toned down and you find satisfaction in "good enough." These are all positive signs of your progress.

My wish for you is that you will use this little book to set yourself free: to transition from seeing your life as a powerless one of victimhood to one that is fulfilling, happy and thriving, even if it was born out of pain.

Thriving

The Role Of Shame

■ ■ ■

Shame is painful self-judgment that you are fundamentally inferior or worthless. This feeling is often implanted early in life in response to traumatic events or abuse. Shame has you assuming responsibility for someone's actions or for the situation in which the harm was done.

Later in life, the cycle of shame is easily activated when you encounter disapproval or failure. You again blame yourself for the situation or abuse, leading you to feel less worthy of anything better.

Some of us pursue drugs, alcohol, or other addictive behaviors to cover up this sense of shame. This eventually backfires, because the addictive substances create a whole other level of pain and self-loathing due to the lack of self-control felt after participating in such behaviors. You then have the pain from the initial shame as well as the pain from the consequences of the self-abusing behavior.

Some may attempt to overcome shame with hard work to prove they are not worthless. Often the money is not enough, or someone gets in the way of their progress. However, the initial shame is still present and is now compounded by the lack of worldly success.

Others attempt to alleviate the shame by gaining the approval and adoration of others. We sacrifice our own wants, needs, and desires so that others will thank and praise us. The praise momentarily relieves the pain, but it never seems to be enough. We become tired and resentful because all our self-sacrifice does not eliminate the pain of our shame.

That deep feeling of not being "ok" or safe is an indicator that our shame has been awakened. While the shame may always be present, you have the capacity to minimize its impact on your life. Forgiving the source of the original pain, learning to stop the behaviors you adopted to cope with the shame and choosing positive behaviors that validate your own worth is what will put you on the road to thriving. Learning to give yourself such validation takes awareness and practice. The tools in this book are designed to help you with that process.

Resources

■ ■ ■

I resisted making this list because I don't know who can help you where you are, but I trust that there is great benefit in the search as well as in the finding. Each individual may bring you a different gem of insight, motivation, and practical principles for change. They point and support you toward the best version of yourself.

You can always begin at your local place of worship. Ask friends or confidants what resources they found to overcome your particular issue. You may also attend a twelve-step group, which provides guiding principles and outlines a course of action for recovery from addiction, compulsion, or other behavioral problems.

Here is a short list of some of the voices who have spoken to me and who have contributed to my own thriving life. You may want to start here, but your mission is to find the voices you can hear. Once you find the voices who speak to you, you will begin to develop a trust that who you are is good, what you want is possible and who you want to become is achievable. Trust the voices who speak to you. They will teach you to trust yourself.

Amanda Gore	*amandagore.com*
Brene Brown	*brenebrown.com*
Byron Katie	*thework.com*
Deepak Chopra	*chopra.com*
Dr. Andrew Weil	*drweil.com*
Dr. Christiane Northrup	*drnorthrup.com*
Dr. Joe Dispenza	*drjoedispenza.com*
Dr. Wayne Dyer	*drwaynedyer.com*
Louise Hay	*louisehay.com*
Melody Beattie	*melodybeattie.com*
SARK	*planetsark.com*
Eckhart Tolle	*eckharttolle.com*
Nick Vujicic	*nickvujicic.com*

About the Author

■ ■ ■

Rebecca Morley holds a master's degree in special education and a master's degree in counseling from the University of South Florida. A Florida-licensed counselor since 2000, she is also a nationally certified counselor with the National Board of Certified Counselors. She has worked professionally in community mental health, faith-based counseling, family restoration, hospice care, and private practice.

Rebecca believes we all have unlimited capacity for growth and expansion. She offers *Thriving: Stepping Into the Life You Want* as a guide to your own happy life.

A percentage of profits will be donated to charity.
You may go to
MYthRIVINGLIfe.ORg
for more information.